Let's Get Moving
on Safari

Emma Lynch

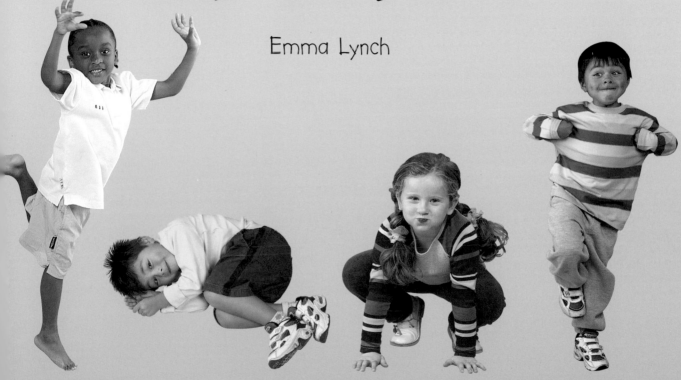

Raintree

Chicago, Illinois

Printed and bound by South China Printing Company.
09 08 07 06 05
10 9 8 7 6 5 4 3 2 1

Library of Congress Cataloging-in-Publication Data:
Lynch, Emma.
  On safari / Emma Lynch.
      p. cm. -- (Let's get moving)
  Includes bibliographical references and index.
  ISBN 1-4109-0867-4 (library binding - hardcover) -- ISBN 1-4109-0872-0 (pbk.)
  1. Human locomotion--Juvenile literature. 2. Animal locomotion--Juvenile literature. 3. Safaris--Juvenile literature. 4. Exercise for children--Juvenile literature. I. Title. II. Series: Lynch, Emma.
Let's get moving.
  QP301.L96 2004
  612.7'6--dc22

                              2004019221

Acknowledgments
The publishers would like to thank the following for permission to reproduce photographs: Alamy pp. **14a** (Magdy Aly), **6a** (Winifried Wisniewski); Corbis pp. **10a** (Tom Brakefield), **16a** (Michael & Patricia Fogden), **5a** (Paul A. Souders); Corbis/ Royalty Free pp. **4a, 7a, 11a, 15a, 17a, 18a, 19a, 20a, 21a, 23**; Getty Images pp. **8a** (Digital Vision), **9a** (photodisc); Harcourt Education Ltd pp. **4b, 5b, 6b, 7b, 8b, 9b, 10b, 11b, 12b, 13b, 14b, 15b, 16b, 17b, 18b, 19b, 20b, 21b, 22** (Tudor Photography); NPL pp. **12a** (Tony Heald), **13a** (Francois Savigny).

Cover photograph reproduced with permission of NHPA/ Daryl Balfour.

Every effort has been made to contact copyright holders of any material reproduced in this book. Any omissions will be rectified in subsequent printings if notice is given to the publishers.

Some words are shown in bold, **like this.** You can find out what they mean by looking in the glossary on page 24.

Contents

Going on Safari

Reach up **high** and stretch your arms out **wide** like a beautiful tree.

swish! swish!

Sway like the grass
in a gentle breeze.

Across the Grassland

Stretch your body and **roar** like a lion.

mane

Rrrrroooooaaarrrr!

Walk like an
elephant swinging
your trunk.

High and Low

Climb high
like a monkey.

Swoop low like a vulture looking for food.

In and Out of Danger

Prowl like a hungry hyena looking for a snack.

Gallop like a zebra—don't look back!

11

Running

Can you run as *fast* as an ostrich?

Run and **jump** like a gazelle.

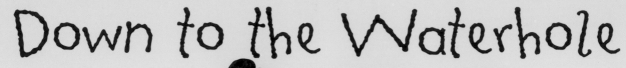

Down to the Waterhole

Follow my leader down to the **waterhole**.

14

Waddle to the water like a happy hippopotamus.

15

At the Water's Edge

Stand on one leg and **balance** like a flamingo.

Can you smile
like a crocodile?

Hunting

Creep through the long grass
like a hunting cheetah.

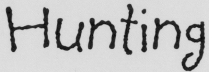

Stop, start, stop, start,
swish, swash, sssshh!

Leap high into the air like a lion to catch your **prey**.

19

Lunchtime

Stretch up to the high leaves like a long-necked giraffe.

Bend down to the ground and root around like a warthog.

Naptime

Even snakes get tired, so curl into a ball and have a rest.

scales

Come back soon for another exciting safari!

Glossary

balance stay upright

prey animal hunted by another animal for food

scales rough skin of a snake

waterhole small lake

Index

Notes for Adults

Let's get moving! explores the many different ways humans can move and encourages children to take part in physical activity. *Let's get moving!* also supports children's growing knowledge and understanding of the wider world, introducing them to different plants and animals and the way they move and grow. Used together, the books will enable comparison of different movements and of a variety of habitats and the animals that live in them.

This book introduces the reader to a range of movements used by animals on the African savannah. It will also help children extend their vocabulary as they hear new words like *swoop* and *prowl*. You may like to introduce and explain other new words yourself, like *species*, *habitat* and *conservation*.

Additional information

Most living things can move. Humans and many other animals have skeletons and muscles to support and protect their bodies and to help them move. Safari often refers to a trip to see animals in their natural habitat. Most trips take place in the African savannah, which is a grassy plain. There is typically a wet and dry season in savannah places with rain in the summer months, and almost completely dry winters.

Follow-up activities

• Can the children think of other animals from the African savannah? Try to copy their movements.
• Select one of the animals mentioned, for example elephants, to do a class project on. Find out about their lifecycles, what they eat, and how they live.
• Draw, paint or make models of the animals that live in the African savannah.

DATE DUE

MAY 27			